D1573021

A JOURNEY WITH FRANCISCO VÁZQUEZ DE CORONADO

STUART A. KALLEN

LERNER PUBLICATIONS ◆ MINNEAPOLIS

Content consultant:
Sarah Chambers, PhD, History, University of Wisconsin, Madison
Professor in the Department of History, University of Minnesota

Lerner Publications Company
A division of Lerner Publishing Group, Inc.
241 First Avenue North
Minneapolis, MN 55401 USA

For reading levels and more information, look up this title at www.lernerbooks.com.

Main body text set in AvenirLTPro 12/18.
Typeface provided by Linotype AG.

Library of Congress Cataloging-in-Publication Data

Names: Kallen, Stuart A., 1955– author.
Title: A journey with Francisco Vázquez de Coronado / Stuart A. Kallen.
Description: Minneapolis : Lerner Publications, 2017. | Series: Primary source explorers | Includes bibliographical references and index.
Identifiers: LCCN 2016010667 (print) | LCCN 2016014174 (ebook) | ISBN 9781512407730 (lb : alk. paper) | ISBN 9781512410969 (eb pdf)
Subjects: LCSH: Coronado, Francisco Vasquez de, 1510–1554—Juvenile literature. | Explorers—America—Biography—Juvenile literature. | Explorers—Spain—Biography—Juvenile literature. | Southwest, New—Discovery and exploration—Spanish—Juvenile literature. | America—Discovery and exploration—Spanish—Juvenile literature.
Classification: LCC E125.V3 K35 2017 (print) | LCC E125.V3 (ebook) | DDC 910.92—dc23

LC record available at http://lccn.loc.gov/2016010667

Manufactured in the United States of America
1-39345-21157-12/16/2016

CONTENTS

 = Denotes primary source

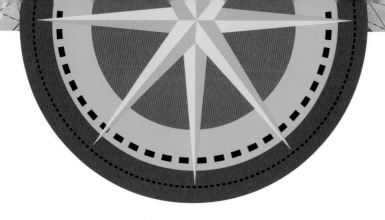

INTRODUCTION
THE SEARCH FOR GOLD

In 1540 Spanish explorer Francisco Vázquez de Coronado was the governor of New Galicia, a province in northern Mexico. Coronado's friend Antonio de Mendoza ruled all of Mexico, then called New Spain. Mendoza and Coronado had heard rumors about the Seven Cities of Cibola. The mythical cities of Cibola were said to be filled with silver, gold, and jewels. And they were supposed to be somewhere in New Spain.

In April 1540, Coronado put together an expedition to find the Seven Cities of Cibola. But after months of travel, Coronado found only deserts and Native villages.

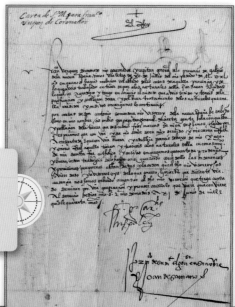

Among those who were literate, letter writing was a main form of communication in the sixteenth century. This letter was addressed to Coronado on June 21, 1540. It is a primary source.

This map was made in 1769 based on the original from 1541. It shows the western coast of New Spain, or Mexico, as it looked in Coronado's time.

As Coronado stated in a letter to Mendoza, "As far as I can judge, it does not appear to me that there is any hope of getting gold or silver, but I trust in God that, if there is any, we shall get our share of it, and it shall not escape us through any lack of diligence in the search."

Coronado's letter is a primary source. Primary sources are documents and objects that make up the raw materials of history. Other primary sources from Coronado's era include reports, drawings, weapons, trade goods, and clothing.

The value of primary sources can be seen in the sentence from Coronado's letter. At the time, Coronado had been searching the sunbaked deserts for nearly four months. The letter shows that Coronado devoted all his time to finding the cities of riches. But he admitted his efforts had failed. Coronado kept hope alive and promised Mendoza he would not abandon his mission.

Although Coronado's letter is more than 475 years old, it opens a window to his journey. Taken with other primary sources of the era, the letter provides a snapshot of a distant time. Coronado was driven to find gold and determined not to give up.

This portrait of Coronado shows what he may have looked like. It was created long after the explorer lived, so it is not a primary source.

CHAPTER 1
BECOMING A GOVERNOR

Francisco Vázquez de Coronado was born in Salamanca, Spain, around 1510. He was the second son of Isabel de Luján. His older brother was named Gonzalo. His father, Juan Vázquez de Coronado, was an upper-class official. He worked for Iñigo López de Mendoza, the governor of Granada, Spain. Mendoza had a son named Antonio, who was friends with Francisco.

Francisco was about eight years old in 1519 when Spanish conquistadores invaded Mexico. Hernán Cortés came to Mexico with about five hundred soldiers. He also recruited Native peoples who were against the ruling Aztecs. Their combined forces conquered the Aztec capital within two years.

The Spaniards renamed the surrounding territory New Spain. In April 1535, Antonio de Mendoza was made viceroy of New Spain. Mendoza asked Coronado to sail to New Spain with him and work as his assistant.

Coronado had been in New Spain less than a year when he married Beatriz de Estrada. She came from a powerful family. The marriage made Coronado rich because of a system called

Antonio de Mendoza appears in this oil painting made in 1535.

encomienda. Under this system, Spanish rulers could force Native people to work for them. However, they could not legally buy and sell the Native people as slaves. The minerals the Native people mined and the foods they produced were taken by the Spanish. Spanish king Charles V gave the rights guaranteed by encomienda to Estrada's family. Coronado received half the wealth through his marriage.

Charles V is depicted in this sixteenth-century portrait. Beatriz de Estrada came into great wealth due to rights Charles V granted to her family, and Coronado inherited some of this wealth when he married her.

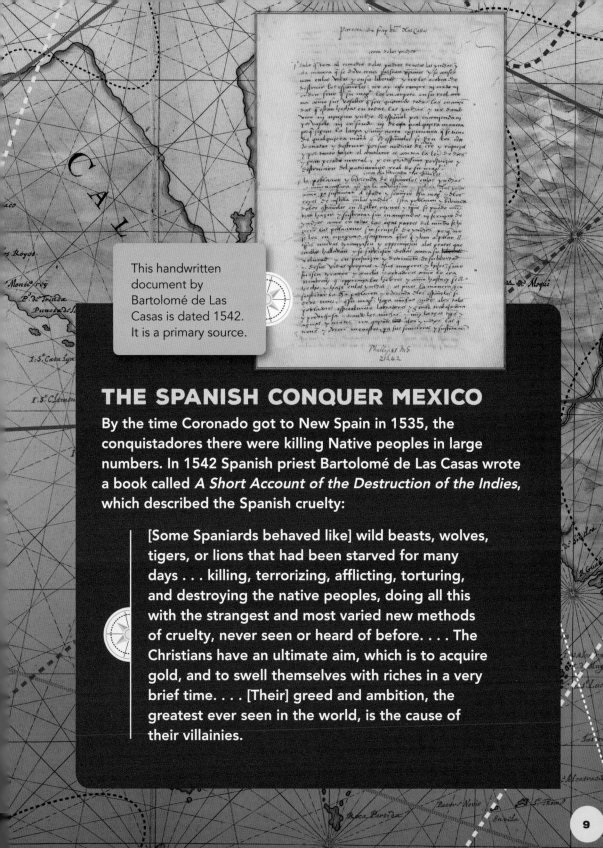

This handwritten document by Bartolomé de Las Casas is dated 1542. It is a primary source.

THE SPANISH CONQUER MEXICO

By the time Coronado got to New Spain in 1535, the conquistadores there were killing Native peoples in large numbers. In 1542 Spanish priest Bartolomé de Las Casas wrote a book called *A Short Account of the Destruction of the Indies*, which described the Spanish cruelty:

> [Some Spaniards behaved like] wild beasts, wolves, tigers, or lions that had been starved for many days . . . killing, terrorizing, afflicting, torturing, and destroying the native peoples, doing all this with the strangest and most varied new methods of cruelty, never seen or heard of before. . . . The Christians have an ultimate aim, which is to acquire gold, and to swell themselves with riches in a very brief time. . . . [Their] greed and ambition, the greatest ever seen in the world, is the cause of their villainies.

INSPECTOR CORONADO

In 1537 labor troubles erupted in and around Mexico City. African slaves and Native encomienda workers revolted at a mine. Mendoza appointed Coronado the official investigator and sent him to look into the situation. Coronado decided four African men were guilty of causing the uprising. The rebels were tortured and killed on Coronado's orders. Mendoza was so pleased that he praised Coronado's role in a letter to King Charles V.

Workers in Mexico's Spanish mines faced many hardships. This undated engraving shows Native workers toiling in a mine by candlelight.

The archaeological site of Sultepec can still be seen near Mexico City.

Mendoza soon gave Coronado another task. There were problems at a mine near the town of Sultepec, west of Mexico City. Owners of the mine were accused of abusing the Native miners. The workers were forced to carry heavy loads without food or rest. The mineowners weren't supposed to abuse the workers, according to rules the Spanish royalty had made about encomienda laborers. Spanish royalty had also ordered mineowners to teach the workers about Christianity. The mineowners hadn't been following through on that order either.

WHAT DO YOU THINK?

How do you think Coronado's wealth affected his attitudes toward the Native people of New Spain?

Coronado looked into the situation. He decided the mineowners were at fault. The matter was turned over to the high court in Mexico City. The mineowners had to pay a fine.

BECOMING GOVERNOR

In 1538 Coronado was assigned another mission. Mendoza sent Coronado to the town of Compostela (present-day Sonora, Mexico). The city was the capital of New Galicia. The territory includes several modern-day states in Mexico, including Jalisco and Nayarit.

A map of Spanish America in 1562 shows New Galicia (present-day Sonora). It is near the top of the map. At that time—as during Coronado's lifetime—the area was sparsely populated compared to now. Modern Sonora is home to more than two million people.

Coronado's mission involved writing a progress report about the governor of New Galicia, Diego Pérez de la Torre. But when Coronado arrived in Compostela, he found that Pérez had died. Since the job was vacant, Coronado took over the governor's duties. In April 1539, Mendoza officially appointed Coronado the governor of New Galicia. After just four years in New Spain, Coronado had risen to a position of great power.

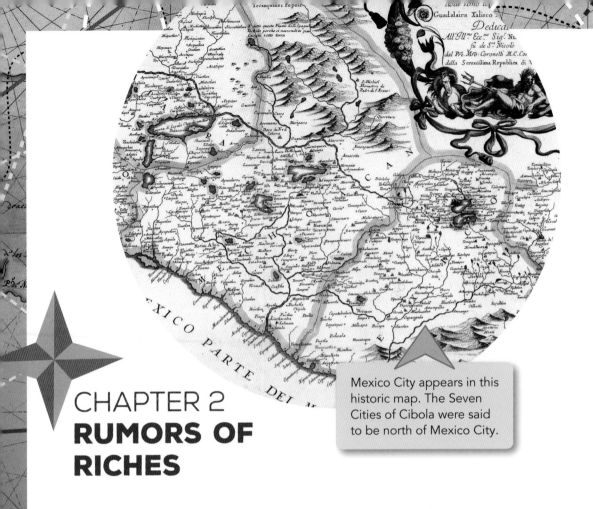

Mexico City appears in this historic map. The Seven Cities of Cibola were said to be north of Mexico City.

CHAPTER 2
RUMORS OF RICHES

When Coronado traveled to Compostela in New Galicia in 1538, he traveled with Friar Marcos de Niza, a Franciscan monk. Friar Marcos went to New Galicia to look into a rumor.

In 1536 some Spanish explorers and an African slave (who spoke some Native languages and served as the men's guide) had arrived in Mexico City with an intriguing claim. The men were the sole survivors of an expedition that had started in Florida in 1527 and ended nine years later in Mexico City. They claimed they'd heard stories that the region they'd passed through was home to the Seven Cities of Cibola. The cities were filled with treasures.

Coronado asked Mexican Native peoples about the cities. Several people told him about a rich land made up of many villages. Coronado wrote a letter telling Mendoza that the people of Cibola wore "gold, emeralds, and other precious stones."

EMERALDS AND JEWELS

In March 1539, Mendoza sent Friar Marcos to search for Cibola near the present-day border between the United States and Mexico. After three months, Friar Marcos returned to Compostela. He wrote a report saying he found the cities of Cibola far to the north.

It is unknown what Friar Marcos really saw. Historians think he may have seen large settlements built by the Zuni people. The settlements were called pueblos and contained adobe homes. They were made from bricks coated with mud.

Coronado was excited by Friar Marcos's report. He left with Friar Marcos for Mexico City to tell Mendoza about the riches of Cibola.

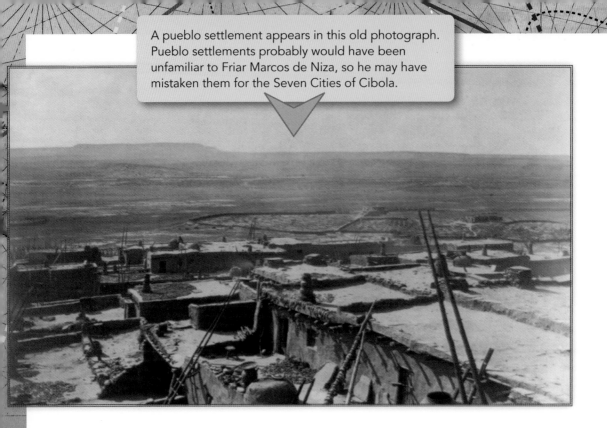

A pueblo settlement appears in this old photograph. Pueblo settlements probably would have been unfamiliar to Friar Marcos de Niza, so he may have mistaken them for the Seven Cities of Cibola.

Coronado and Mendoza put together an army to conquer Cibola. The men would need money to pay soldiers and to buy food, weapons, and other supplies. Coronado funded part of the mission with the money he gained through his marriage. Mendoza also added money to the mission. They believed they would make large profits after they conquered Cibola and seized its treasures.

In June 1539, Coronado wrote to Spain's King Charles V asking for permission to travel to the northern lands. A king's assistant named Francisco García de Loaysa wrote back to Coronado. The official instructed Coronado to spread Christianity: "Through your excellent efforts you will bring the natives of that province under our sway . . . and will bring them into the knowledge of the holy catholic faith."

The conquistador Bernal Díaz del Castillo later wrote a book about Spain's role in Mexico. He was more honest about Coronado and other Spanish explorers: "We came here to serve God and the King, and also to get rich."

GATHERING AN ARMY

Coronado gathered an expedition at Compostela on February 23, 1540. There were about 280 Spanish soldiers and several monks including Friar Marcos. The crew also included about 1,300 Native peoples and servants. The soldiers carried pole weapons called lances. They were armed with swords, crossbows, rifles called harquebuses, and much more.

This engraving of conquistador Bernal Díaz del Castillo was made in the sixteenth century.

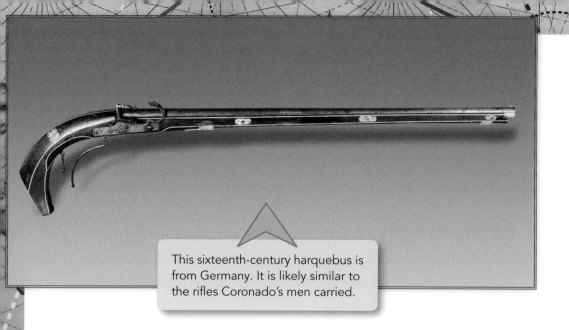

This sixteenth-century harquebus is from Germany. It is likely similar to the rifles Coronado's men carried.

The sound of trumpets filled the air when Coronado took his place at the head of the army. He was confident he could conquer the Native peoples and convert them to Christianity. Above all, Coronado was sure he would find Cibola and become the richest man in New Spain.

WHAT DO YOU THINK?

What role did religion play in Coronado's quest to find the Seven Cities of Cibola?

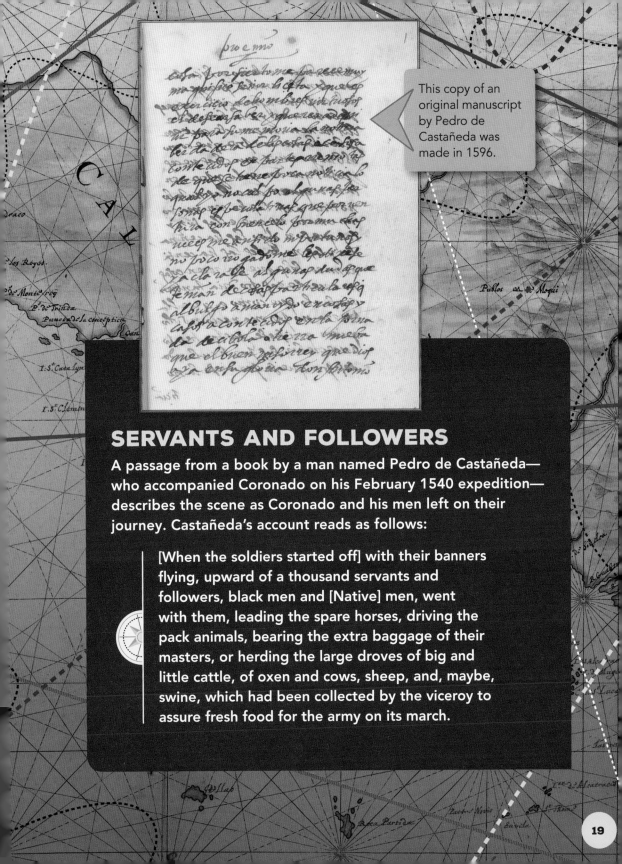

This copy of an original manuscript by Pedro de Castañeda was made in 1596.

SERVANTS AND FOLLOWERS

A passage from a book by a man named Pedro de Castañeda—who accompanied Coronado on his February 1540 expedition—describes the scene as Coronado and his men left on their journey. Castañeda's account reads as follows:

[When the soldiers started off] with their banners flying, upward of a thousand servants and followers, black men and [Native] men, went with them, leading the spare horses, driving the pack animals, bearing the extra baggage of their masters, or herding the large droves of big and little cattle, of oxen and cows, sheep, and, maybe, swine, which had been collected by the viceroy to assure fresh food for the army on its march.

The cathedral of Culiacán is brightly illuminated in this modern photo.

CHAPTER 3
THE QUEST FOR GOLD

In early March 1540, Coronado was eager to find Cibola. But the thousands of people and animals on the expedition were having a tough time. Trails were narrow. There were many rivers to cross. The servants were so loaded down with equipment that they lagged far behind the soldiers on horseback. The army could move only about 10 miles (16 kilometers) a day.

On March 28, the expedition arrived at the Spanish outpost of Culiacán. By then Coronado realized his expedition was too large. There was not enough food and water on the route ahead to support all the soldiers and servants. Coronado decided to leave the weaker members of his crew behind.

On April 22, Coronado left Culiacán with seventy-five horsemen, twenty-five foot soldiers, and a small group of servants. Friar Marcos and three other monks were also part of the group. For more than a month, the expedition pushed through northern Mexico and into eastern Arizona.

The situation grew desperate as cold weather slowed the men in the White Mountains of Arizona. Coronado wrote that the hard trail troubled the soldiers and that several servants fell down and died. This was a huge loss to the expedition. Horses also struggled to survive.

The soldiers had some corn to eat, but supplies ran very low. Some were so hungry they ate plants along the trail. The plants were poisonous, and several soldiers died. Coronado described

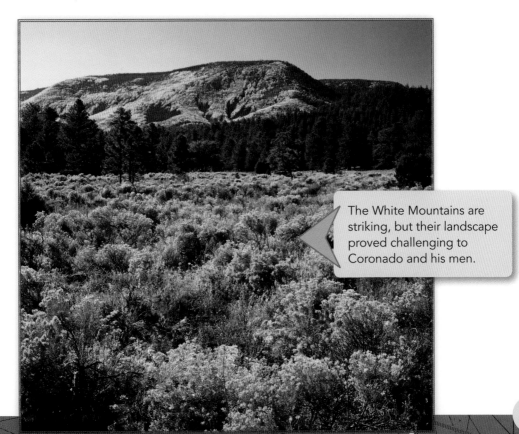

The White Mountains are striking, but their landscape proved challenging to Coronado and his men.

conditions in a letter to Mendoza: "I entered the borders of the wilderness [and found] . . . a worse way through mountains and more dangerous passages than we had experienced previously. The horses were so tired that they were not equal to it, so in this last desert we lost more horses than before."

"CRUMPLED" VILLAGE

By early July, the expedition was within 5 miles (8 km) of several towns Friar Marcos had called Cibola. The soldiers set up camp, but local Native peoples soon discovered them and tried to scare them away. The Native peoples circled the camp, yelling through the night. The soldiers scrambled to defend themselves from a likely attack. Some were so scared they put the saddles on their horses backward.

On July 7, Coronado rode near the first of the Seven Cities of Cibola. It was a village the Zuni called Hawikuh. The village of about five hundred people had adobe houses surrounded by high walls. Castañeda described Hawikuh: "It is a little, unattractive village, looking as if it had been crumpled all up together. . . . It is a village of about 200 warriors, is three and four stories high, with the houses small and having only a few rooms, and without a courtyard." When the soldiers saw that Hawikuh had no treasures, they cursed and shouted at Friar Marcos.

WHAT DO YOU THINK?

How do you think the Zuni interpreted the situation when they saw Coronado's soldiers surrounding their village bearing weapons?

This work of art shows Coronado's men arriving at Hawikuh.

"SEVEN LITTLE VILLAGES"

While the village had no riches, the Native peoples had supplies of corn and other foods. Driven by hunger, Coronado decided to attack Hawikuh to get the food. But his soldiers were so weak they could barely stand. Many had trouble shooting their crossbows and muskets. Coronado led the charge, riding near the walls around the village. Native warriors fought back by pelting him with stones. As Coronado wrote in a letter to Mendoza, "[The warriors] knocked me down to the ground twice with countless great stones which they threw down from above and if I had not been protected by the very good headpiece which I wore, I think that the outcome would have been bad for me."

Zuni gardens such as these would have looked like treasures to Coronado's hungry soldiers.

Coronado was shot through the foot with an arrow and was rescued. The soldiers fought on, and they were able to capture the village. But Coronado had to face reality. There was no treasure. Coronado explained the situation to Mendoza:

> [Friar Marcos] has not told the truth in a single thing that he said, but everything is the reverse of what he said, except the name of the city and the large stone houses.

The Seven Cities [of Cibola] are seven little villages. . . .
You may be assured that if there had been all the riches
and treasures of the world, I could not have done more
[to capture them].

Friar Marcos was sent back to Mexico City in disgrace. But
Coronado refused to leave. He decided to continue his search
for treasures no matter how hard the task.

CORONADO DESCRIBES HAWIKUH

Coronado described the village of Hawikuh, which his men
had attacked in an attempt to get food, in detail in a letter to
Antonio de Mendoza. The following is part of this letter:

Although [the houses] are not decorated with
turquoises, nor made of lime nor of good
bricks . . . they are very good houses, with
three and four and five stories, where there are
very good apartments and good rooms with
[hallways], and some very good rooms under
ground . . . which are made for winter, and are
something like a sort of hot baths. The ladders
which they have for their houses are all moveable
and portable, which are taken up and placed
wherever they please.

The Grand Canyon is aglow with sunlight in this photo. The Colorado River can be seen flowing through the canyon on the left side of the image. Coronado's scouting party became the first Europeans to see both the canyon and the river.

CHAPTER 4
TO KANSAS AND BACK

Coronado found no riches in Cibola, but he remained there with his expedition. Coronado asked the Zuni where he might find cities filled with gold and jewels. The Zuni told him of a river where giants were said to live. Coronado sent a scouting party to the river on August 25, 1540.

The twenty-five soldiers were led by García López de Cárdenas. The men walked for nearly three weeks before seeing a canyon with a river flowing through it below. The group spent three days looking for a trail down to the river, but they could not find one. Although Cárdenas did not know it, his men were the first Europeans to see the Grand Canyon and the Colorado River.

THE TIGUEX WAR

In September Coronado realized his soldiers would not have enough food to spend the winter in Cibola. He moved his crew to Tiguex, where the weather was warmer and there was more food. Tiguex was on the Rio Grande near modern Bernalillo. It was made up of about twenty pueblos. The people who lived there were of the Tiwa tribe.

Coronado's men clashed with the Tiwa. Soldiers stole blankets and coats off the backs of Native men. The Tiwa attacked the expedition's horses and mules, killing about fifty animals. This caused Coronado to declare war on the Tiwa.

This American Indian ceremonial figure was painted around 1500.

The Tiguex War lasted from January to March 1541. The Spaniards attacked a village called Arenal, and a battle followed. Coronado's men set Arenal on fire. They killed hundreds of Native peoples as they tried to escape the flames. About two hundred Tiwa were captured and burned at the stake. Hundreds of Native peoples were killed, and their villages were destroyed.

ANOTHER RUMOR OF GOLD

After the fighting ended, a Native prisoner the Spaniards called the Turk told Coronado about a village called Quivira, in modern-day Kansas. The place was ruled by a king who slept under a tree filled with golden ornaments. The people were so rich that even the servants ate from gold dishes. Coronado learned that Quivira was far to the northeast.

No gold hung from the trees in Quivira, but it was rich with open land and native plants and grasses.

Many of the Spanish soldiers thought the Turk was lying. They believed he was trying to lead them into the wilderness where they would get lost and die. But Coronado had failed to find gold and had spent all his money looking for Cibola. He was extremely eager to return home with gold.

On April 23, 1541, the Coronado expedition left for Quivira. The Turk led the way. The crew traveled through eastern New Mexico and into northern Texas and the eastern Oklahoma Panhandle. The grass there grew more than 6 feet (1.8 meters) high, and there were no trails to follow. The soldiers were frightened by the endless sea of grass. But they were amazed by the herds of buffalo—animals they had never seen before. Coronado called the buffalo humpbacked cows.

The sight of grazing buffalo amazed and startled Coronado and his men.

FINDING QUIVIRA

In the middle of August, Coronado reached Quivira. Several hundred Wichita tribe members lived there in straw houses, and they hunted buffalo. Coronado was once again troubled by what he found. Quivira had no gold, silver, or jewels. Coronado gave orders to his men to kill the Turk for leading his expedition astray.

These straw homes inhabited by the Wichita closely match a description Coronado gave of the dwellings in 1541.

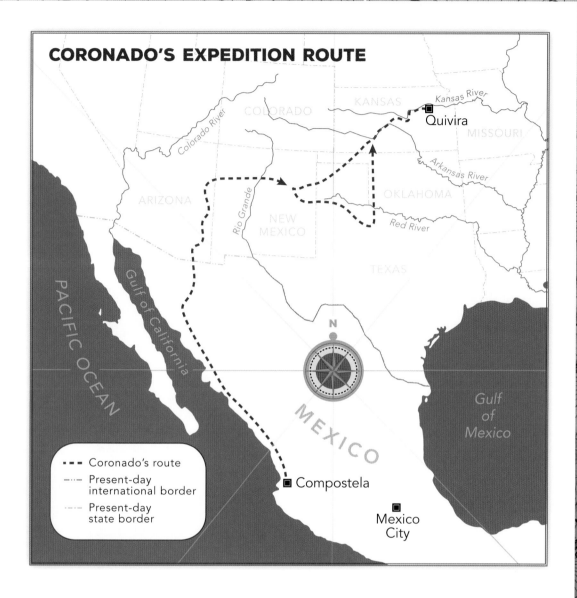

CORONADO'S EXPEDITION ROUTE

Legend:
- ▪▪▪ Coronado's route
- ─··─ Present-day international border
- ─·─ Present-day state border

    Winter was coming, and Coronado decided to give up his search for gold. On October 20, 1541, Coronado wrote a report about his mission to the king, admitting he had failed: "What I am sure of is that there is not any gold nor any other metal in all that country, and the [grand cities] of which they had told me are nothing but little villages."

Coronado returned to New Galicia in 1542. His money was gone. The viceroy of New Spain believed Coronado was a failure and eventually took away his title as governor of New Galicia. Coronado lived out the last years of his life in Mexico City. On September 22, 1554, he died from an unnamed disease. He was about forty-four years old. While Coronado never found cities of gold, he was the first European to explore the deserts and plains of what is now the United States of America.

WHAT DO YOU THINK?

Coronado was determined to gain money and power, even if his quest to do so had dire consequences for those he encountered on his journey. Do you think society places a similar value on power and wealth today? Or have our views changed?

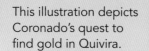
This illustration depicts Coronado's quest to find gold in Quivira.

LED ASTRAY

After failing to find gold in Quivira, Coronado wrote a letter to Spain's King Charles V. Coronado said his American Indian guides led him astray in hopes he would die in the wilderness:

> The account [the guides] gave me was false, because they wanted to persuade me to go there with the whole force, believing that as the way was through such uninhabited deserts, and from the lack of water, they would get us where we and our horses would die of hunger. And the guides confessed this, and said they had done it by the advice and orders of the natives of these provinces.

TIMELINE

1510 Francisco Vásquez de Coronado is born in Salamanca, Spain, around this time.

1519 Spanish conquistador Hernán Cortés arrives in Mexico.

1521 Cortés and his soldiers conquer the Aztecs and name the land New Spain.

1535 Coronado moves to New Spain to work as an assistant to Viceroy Antonio de Mendoza.

1536 Coronado marries Beatriz de Estrada.

1537 Coronado puts down a slave revolt at a silver mine southwest of Mexico City.

1539 Coronado is appointed governor of New Galicia.

1540 On February 23, the Coronado expedition marches north in search of the Seven Cities of Cibola. In July he finds the city of Cibola, but it is a plain Zuni village with no treasure.

1541 Between January and March, Coronado's army fights the Tiwa of Tiguex, killing hundreds. In August he and thirty soldiers ride into Quivira but find no gold or jewels.

1542 Coronado is back in New Galicia, having failed to find cities filled with gold.

1544 Coronado is removed as governor of New Galicia.

1554 On September 22, Coronado dies from an unknown disease at about the age of forty-four.

SOURCE NOTES

5   George Parker Winship, ed., *The Coronado Expedition, 1540–1542* (Washington, DC: Smithsonian Institution, 1896), 563.

9   Bartolomé de Las Casas, *The Devastation of the Indies: A Brief Account* (New York: Seabury, 1974), 39.

15 Richard Flint and Shirley Cushing Flint, eds. *Documents of the Coronado Expedition, 1539–1542* (Albuquerque: University of New Mexico, 2005), 31.

16 Francisco García de Loaysa, "Spain Authorizes Coronado's Conquest in the Southwest, 1540," Gilder Lehrman Institute of American History, accessed July 12, 2016, http://www.gilderlehrman.org/history-by-era/exploration/resources/spain-authorizes-coronado%E2%80%99s-conquest-southwest-1540.

17 Paul Horgan, *Great River: The Rio Grande in North American History*, vol. 1 (Middletown, CT: Wesleyan University Press, 1994), 239.

19 Winship, *Coronado Expedition*, 378.

22 Ibid., 555.

22 Ibid., 483.

23 Ibid., 557.

24–25 Ibid., 558.

25 Ibid.

31 Ibid., 583.

33 Ibid.

GLOSSARY

conquistador: the Spanish word for *conqueror*, used to describe the soldiers who arrived in the New World and took control of lands occupied by Native people

encomienda: a system that allowed Spanish rulers to force Native people to work for them but did not allow the Spanish to buy and sell Native people as slaves

expedition: a journey or voyage undertaken by a group of people with a specific purpose

Franciscan: a friar, sister, or other member of a Christian religious order founded in 1209 by Saint Francis of Assisi

harquebus: an early type of rifle that was muzzle-loaded. Harquebuses were used between the fifteenth and seventeenth centuries.

mythical: based on or described in a myth

rumor: an unlikely or unclear story or report

viceroy: a person who rules a colony on behalf of a king or queen

SELECTED BIBLIOGRAPHY

Aiton, Arthur Scott. *Antonio de Mendoza, First Viceroy of New Spain.* Durham, NC: Duke University Press, 1927.

Flint, Richard, and Shirley Cushing Flint, eds. *Documents of the Coronado Expedition, 1539–1542.* Albuquerque: University of New Mexico, 2005.

Winship, George Parker, ed. *The Coronado Expedition, 1540–1542.* Washington, DC: Smithsonian Institution, 1896.

FURTHER INFORMATION

DesertUSA: Coronado Expedition
http://www.desertusa.com/desert-trails/coronado-expedition-quivira.html
This site provides a detailed account of Coronado's quest for gold and treasure in the Southwest.

Farndon, John. *How to Live Like an Aztec Priest*. Minneapolis: Hungry Tomato, 2017. Join a fun exploration of Aztec religion and government in the decades before the Spanish invaded Mexico.

Itinerary of the Coronado Expeditions, 1527–1547
http://www.library.arizona.edu/exhibits/swetc/jour/front.1_div.4.html
This site provides a month-by-month account of Coronado's life, his travels to New Spain, and his expeditions in search of Cibola and Quivira.

Lowery, Linda. *Native Peoples of the Southwest*. Minneapolis: Lerner Publications, 2017. Lowery explores the lives of American Indians who lived in New Mexico, Arizona, and elsewhere in the Southwest before and after the arrival of Europeans.

Ramen, Fred. Hernán Cortés: *The Conquest of Mexico and the Aztec Empire*. New York: Cavendish Square, 2015. Ramen describes how Cortés conquered the Native peoples of Mexico and paved the way for Spanish rulers like Coronado to take control of the region.

LERNER

Expand learning beyond the printed book. Download free, complementary educational resources for this book from our website, www.lerneresource.com.

SOURCE

INDEX

PHOTO ACKNOWLEDGMENTS

The images in this book are used with the permission of: Library of Congress Geography and Map Division, background map; Gilder Lehrman Institute of American History, New York, NY, p. 4; courtesy of the John Carter Brown Library at Brown University (CC BY-NC-ND 4.0), p. 5; © Look and Learn/Bridgeman Images, p. 6; The Granger Collection, New York, p. 7; © Musee des Beaux-Arts, Lille, France/Bridgeman Images, p. 8; Library of Congress Rare Book and Special Collections Division Jay I. Kislak Collection (2007574376), p. 9; © North Wind Picture Archives, pp. 10, 24; © Charles Mahaux/AGF Srl/Alamy, p. 11; © Photo Researchers/Alamy, p. 14; Wikimedia Commons (PD), p. 15; Library of Congress (LC-USZ62-89026), p. 16; © Private Collection/Ken Welsh/Bridgeman Images, p. 17; National Park Service Photo/Darryl Herring, p.18; The New York Public Library, p. 19; © Brian Overcast/Alamy, p. 20; © Morey Milbradt/Alamy, p. 21; artwork by Nevin Kempthorne, courtesy of the National Park Service, p. 23; © Tondafoto/Dreamstime.com, p. 26; © Nancy Carter/North Wind Picture Archives, p. 27; Tony Ifland/US Fish and Wildlife Service, p. 28; © Michael Rosebrock/Shutterstock.com, p.29; © Stock Sales WGBH/Scala/Art Resource, NY, p. 30; © Laura Westlund/Independent Picture Service, p. 31; ©Bettmann/Getty Images, p. 33.

Cover: © North Wind Picture Archives/Alamy (main); Library of Congress Geography and Map Division (map).